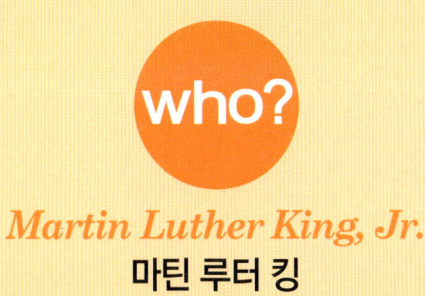

who?

Martin Luther King, Jr.
마틴 루터 킹

Biography Comic
who? ❿ Martin Luther King, Jr.

초판 1쇄 인쇄 2011년 4월 8일
초판 1쇄 발행 2011년 4월 15일

글 안형모
그림 스튜디오 청비
번역 채드 워커
감수 김수희
펴낸이 김선식

Chief Story Creator 김정미
Story Creator 채정은
Design Creator 김경민
Marketing Creator 신문수

Brand Creative Story Team 김정미, 채정은, 박혜연
Creative Design Dept. 최부돈, 황정민, 김태수, 조혜상, 이성희, 김경민
Creative Marketing Dept. 모계영, 이주화, 김하늘, 신문수
       Communication Team 서선행, 김선준, 박혜원, 전아름
       Contents Rights Team 이정순, 김미영
New Business Team 우재오
Creative Management Team 김성자, 김미현, 김유미, 정연주, 서여주, 권송이
Outsourcing 김혜령

펴낸곳 (주)다산북스
주소 서울시 마포구 서교동 395-27번지
전화 02-702-1724(기획편집) 02-703-1725(마케팅) 02-704-1724(경영지원)
팩스 02-703-2219
이메일 dasanbooks@hanmail.net
홈페이지 www.dasanbooks.com
출판등록 2005년 12월 23일 제313-2005-00277호

필름 출력 스크린그래픽센타 **종이** 월드페이퍼(주) **인쇄·제본** (주)현문

ISBN 978-89-6370-523-1 14740
SET 978-89-6370-438-8

who?
Martin Luther King, Jr.
마틴 루터 킹

글 안형모 | 그림 **스튜디오 청비** | 번역 **채드 워커** | 감수 **김수희**

Dasan Kid

Martin Luther King, Jr.

American activist, January 15, 1929~April 4, 1968

In 1986, the United States Congress instituted a national holiday to honor an individual. As one of only four federal holidays created to honor an individual person, the holiday was created to commemorate the birthday of Reverend Martin Luther King, Jr, who devoted his life to improving civil rights for African-Americans.

The widely respected Reverend King was born in 1929 in the city of Atlanta.At that time in the heavily segregated southern U.S., Many African-American, faced with institutionalized racial discrimination.

Reverend King read the works of famous scholars and researched ways to effectively communicate the plight of African-Americans. Then, after hearing a speech by Gandhi he learned about non-violent resistance. Gandhi's teaching--that violence can never be used regardless of the situation and that the only path to happiness for all is through peaceful resistance based on love--greatly inspired Reverend King.

One day, an African-American woman named Rosa Parks was arrested for refusing to give up her seat to a white person on a bus. Thoroughly following Gandhi's spirit of non-violent resistance, Reverend King led a bus boycott, resulting in blacks gaining the right to ride buses freely.

He subsequently garnered the praise of many blacks, elevating him to leader of the civil rights movement. He was frequently arrested and restrained by the police, and was forced to live a life of fear amid threats by racial terrorists.

But King remained undaunted because he firmly believed the day would come when whites and blacks could live together in peace. King's complete embrace of non-violent protest had a powerful impact on not only blacks, but also on many white Americans as well. Support grew for Reverend King's efforts, for which he was granted the Nobel Peace Prize. He provided a ray of hope for the many blacks who had suffered for so long.

마틴 루터 킹

미국의 인권 운동가, 1929년 1월 15일~1968년 4월 4일

1986년 미국 연방 의회는 초대 대통령인 조지 워싱턴 이후 처음으로 개인의 탄생일을 국경일로 삼았습니다. 바로 흑인 인권의 향상을 위해 평생을 바 친 마틴 루터 킹 목사의 탄생을 기리는 날입니다.

많은 사람들이 존경하는 인물로 꼽는 킹 목사는 1929년 미국 남부의 애틀랜타에서 태어났습니다. 인종 차별이 심했던 미국 남부 지방에서 흑인으로 산다는 것은 매우 고통스러운 일이었습니다.

킹 목사는 유명한 학자들의 책을 읽으며 흑인들의 생각을 효과적으로 전달할 수 있는 방법에 대해 연구했습니다. 그러다 한 강연에서 간디의 비폭력 저항주의에 대해 알게 됩니다. 어떠한 경우에도 폭력을 사용해서는 안 되며 사랑을 바탕으로 한 평화로운 투쟁만이 모두가 행복해질 수 있는 길이라는 이 주장은 킹 목사에게 큰 감흥을 주었습니다.

그러던 어느 날, 로자 파크스라는 한 흑인 여성이 버스 안에서 백인에게 자리를 양보하지 않아 체포되는 사건이 발생합니다. 킹 목사는 철저하게 간디의 비폭력 저항주의 정신을 따르며 버스 안타기 운동을 진행하여 흑인들도 자유롭게 버스를 이용할 권리를 얻어 냅니다.

이후 킹 목사는 많은 흑인들의 존경을 받으며 인권 운동의 지도자로 부상합니다. 이후 경찰에 체포, 구속되는 일이 빈번하게 발생했으며, 심지어 테러의 위협 속에 불안한 나날을 보내야만 했습니다.

하지만 킹 목사는 이에 굴하지 않았습니다. 그에게는 언젠가 흑인과 백인이 함께 어우러져 살아가는 세상이 올 것이라는 확고한 믿음이 있었기 때문입니다. 철저하게 비폭력 투쟁을 하는 킹 목사의 일관된 모습에 마침내 모든 흑인은 물론 백인들까지도 감동을 하게 됩니다. 킹 목사는 사람들의 지지를 받으며 노벨 평화상을 수상하였고 고통으로 신음하던 많은 흑인들에게 희망의 등불이 되어 주었습니다.

이 책을 만든 사람들

글 · 안형모

어린이들의 꿈을 키워 주는 재미있고 유익한 만화를 만들기 위해 즐겁게 작업하고 있습니다. 인물 이야기를 통해 위인들의 성공적인 업적보다는 성공에 이르기까지 과정과 노력을 담기 위해 노력합니다. 『천추태후』, 『통째로 한국사 1, 2』, 『호동왕자와 낙랑공주』 등의 만화 시나리오를 썼습니다.

그림 · 스튜디오 청비

기발한 상상력을 바탕으로 새롭고 재미있는 콘텐츠를 만들어 내는 만화 창작 집단입니다. 어린이들이 책을 읽고 큰 꿈을 품기를 바라는 마음으로 즐겁게 작업하고 있습니다. 작품으로 『성철 스님』, 『아 다르고 어 다른 우리말 101가지』, 『반기문 유엔 사무총장의 꿈과 도전』 등이 있습니다.

번역 · 채드 워커 (Chad Walker)

미국 텍사스 오스틴에서 심리학과 일본어를 전공했습니다. 일본으로 건너가 10년 간 살았고 이후 한국과 중국을 오가며 한 · 중 · 일의 동아시아 문화를 비교 연구하고 있습니다. 현재는 연세대학교 국어국문학과 박사 과정 중에 있습니다. 옮긴 책으로 『한국어 교육을 위한 한국어 연어사전』, 『한국인의 가치 문화』, 『속성 한국어』 등이 있습니다.

감수 · 김수희

연세대학교에서 역사를 전공했습니다. 이후 한국뿐 아니라 일본, 미국에서 한국어, 일본어, 영어를 가르쳐 왔으며 부모를 위한 영어교육용 책을 썼습니다. 영어교육채널 EBSe '엄마표 영어특강'에서 강의를 하며 홈스쿨, 알파벳과 파닉스, 다차원 테마 영어 수업 기법을 알리고 있습니다. 전국 각지에서 어린이 영어 교육에 대한 강연을 하며 창의적이고 열정적인 교수법으로 영어를 배우고자 하는 어린이와 부모들에게 많은 도움을 주고 있습니다.

Martin Luther King, Jr.

After Martin Luther King, Jr.'s death, citizens of the United States pay tribute to him every third Monday of which month?

a. January
b. March
c. May

Answer: a

Contents

01 The Brightest Jewel in the World

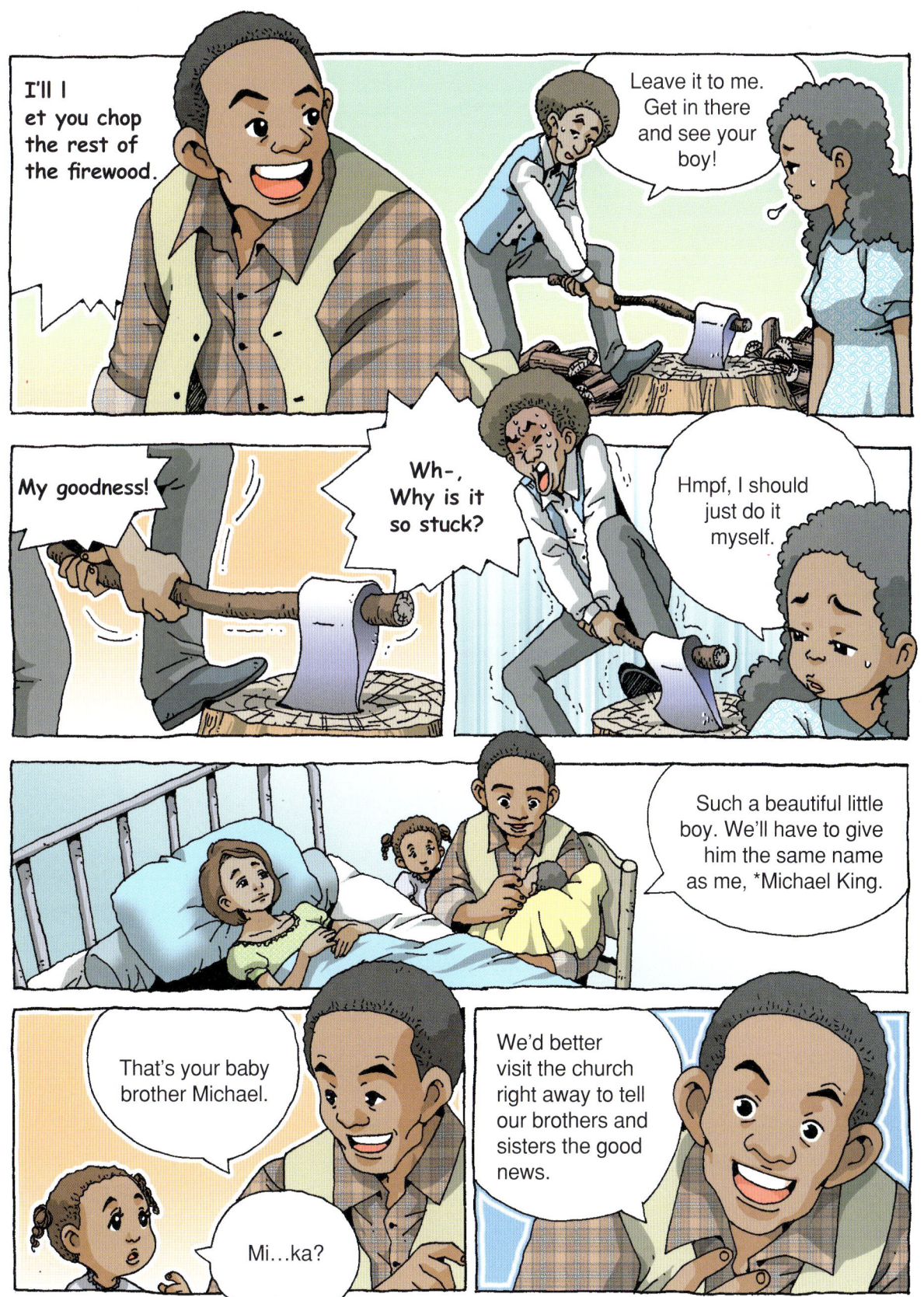

*When Martin Luther King was five his father changed both of their names from "Michael" to "Martin."

11

Dear! Shouldn't we first say a prayer of thanks?

Yes, you're right!

Martin Luther King was born on January 15, 1929, in the southern U.S. city of Atlanta, Georgia.

Thank you for blessing us with our precious boy.

His father, Martin Luther King, Sr., was the minister of Ebenezer Baptist Church.

We pray that this boy may live a peaceful life under the Lord's watchful eye. Please protect him.

He had grown up as the son of a poor tenant farmer. However, no matter how hard he worked, he could never improve his livelihood, so he left home to live in Atlanta.

He labored as a construction worker during the day, while at night he attended school, studying diligently to become a preacher.

And they say at night he goes to study? Amazing.

He was married to Alberta, the daughter of the minister of Ebenezer Baptist Church, and soon after his wedding, he started to preach there himself.

I now pronounce you man and wife. Congratulations.

With a dignified personality and always taking a stand against injustice, he became known as Daddy King.

You've been through a lot, Alberta!

It was all worth it.

You should get some good rest.

Ouch! My hand!

Crack

Oops, I'm sorry.

This is my Father's world~

Six years later,
at Ebenezer Church.

Martin had a younger brother, Alfred Daniel (known as A.D.),
and an older sister, Christine. Together they grew up happily
surrounded by the love of their parents.

the birds their
carols raise,
the morning light
the lily white

Martin, let's go buy
you some new shoes
for your entrance
ceremony!

Martin! Dad's
calling you.

Oh yeah, that's
me. Ever since my
name was changed
I get confused
sometimes.
Hehe!

When Martin was five, his father changed his
son's name from Michael to Martin Luther,
meaning Martin's official full name was now
Martin Luther King.

Okay,
I'll be right down!

14

Because tomorrow's the first day of school, we're going to buy me some new shoes.

Wow, that's great!

See you later.

Have fun! See you when you get back.

1929, the year Martin Luther King was born, marked the beginning of the Great Depression. It was a time of increasing unemployment and economic hardship.

I've got money, so why won't you sell me bread?

I told you we're out of flour and can't make any more. I'm very sorry.

For Martin, who had been raised in better economic times and had never experienced such hardship, the sight of people forming long lines to receive food rations was shocking.

What were all those people doing back there?

They were lining up to buy bread. These days the economy is bad, and many people are unable to buy food.

Hey! That bench is for whites. You have to get up!

The seats for blacks are over there toward the back. Go there to sit.

There's even discrimination here.

If I can't sit on this bench, I won't be buying any shoes here! Let's go, Martin.

What?

Suit yourself! All shops have only certain seats for blacks. They're all the same!

That's the way it is.

Dad, blacks and whites can't sit together?

Even though President Lincoln issued his Emancipation Proclamation many years ago, a few years later whites created Jim Crow laws that have allowed them to continue discriminating against blacks.

Blacks cannot go to a downtown shopping center and buy a hamburger, even if they have money.

Even on buses, the seats for whites and blacks are separate.

Blacks can't attend the same schools as whites, they can't go swimming at pools, and they can't go to parks or theaters where white people are.

Even bathrooms are divided into those for whites and those for blacks.

I don't understand. Did we do something bad to white people?

No. Sorry, son... out of anger I have said too much.

That's an example of what I was talking about earlier. That's the way things are.

Yes, Dad.

Thus, Martin Luther King was introduced to the discrimination existing between blacks and whites.

Soon afterward, he personally experienced racial discrimination when he met with his closest friends.

Where are your new shoes?

We couldn't buy any.

We waited for you to return so we could play, and now you're just going back inside?

What did you say to Martin?

Well...

Even after Martin grows up, I doubt things will be any different.

So I figured it was best he went ahead and learned how blacks must live in society.

But I worry that he'll start to hate white people.

Martin! Let's go get you some shoes.

Find a pair that you like.

Okay, Mom!

Ouch!

?

How dare that little black kid step on my foot!

I would do no such thing.

24

Martin was sad to lose his close friend for the sole reason that he was black.

No, it's not bad at all, Martin. What's bad are the people who discriminate based on skin color.

Through these experiences, Martin gradually began to hate white people.

They said I can't play with Tom anymore. Is having black skin a bad thing?

But, even if white people treat you poorly, you've got to treat them with dignity. Okay?

You've got a shiny jewel hidden inside of you that can never be replaced by anything else in the world. Never forget this fact, and always be proud to be you.

Martin's mother, Alberta Williams King, would lovingly comfort Martin whenever he was hurt by what someone said.

25

Take to heart what your mother just said.

Grandmom?

Doing so will help you immensely in your life.

Huge riots once occurred here in Atlanta.

There will never be a world where blacks and whites are equal.

You blacks will forever be slaves.

Please, just leave us alone!!

26

Dreaming of Becoming a Minister

02

 Track 10 ▶

Martin! What are you reading so intently there? Are they interesting?

Aha.

The life story of Harriet Tubman, who fought for the freedom of blacks, and the great black orator Fredrick Douglas.

I also want to help out blacks who are suffering, just like they did.

Martin loved to read books, and he thought about things more deeply than his peers. He was also known for being a good speaker.

Blacks seem to be living in very poor situations.

Most still get treated inhumanely and live in run-down, cramped houses.

What's gotten into your head lately? Go on, speak up!

Yes, sir. I've been…

When I consider all of creation in the vast universe, I wonder if we truly measure up to any kind of divine standard, being as imperfect as we are and,…

WOW~

Ha ha! You've been studying just fine, I see!

Alright, let's start class then.

I have no idea what that boy's talking about.

30

Democracy cannot blossom in a country where there are people who can't read and are ignored by society.

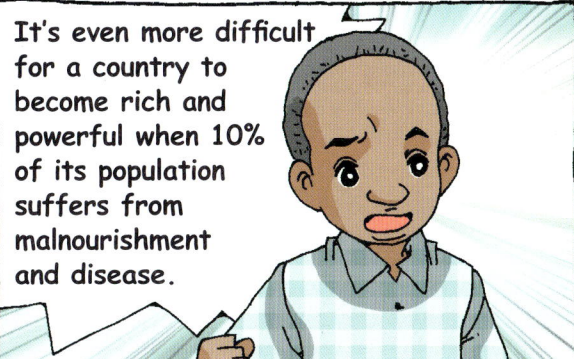

It's even more difficult for a country to become rich and powerful when 10% of its population suffers from malnourishment and disease.

Freedom benefits everyone. Freedom does not discriminate, being favorable to some but unfavorable to others!

Bravo! Incredible!

Martin won 2nd place at the speech contest.

However, on the way home Martin had a horrible experience he would never forget.

See, didn't I say you'd do great? Ha ha ha!

I'm still a bit overwhelmed by it all.

Darn, there aren't any empty seats.

Hey! There aren't any seats available for whites, so you two in the back need to get up.

Didn't you hear what the driver said? Out of the way.

It's not fair to give up our seats just because we're black after paying the same fare to ride the bus. I won't get up.

Looks like I'll have to call the police.

!

Go on, Get up, Martin.

No, I don't want to give up my seat.

Martin, why are you fighting the law?

Martin found the answer to his question when he went to work at a tobacco plantation to make money for school.

You look like you're still in high school, so why are you working here?

I need to make money to pay for my college tuition.

We're not that bad off, but I want to take the burden off my parents as much as possible.

That's very admirable.

What?

You're surely thirsty, so have some water before you go.

But sir! I'm black, so why are you being so kind to me?

This is precisely the reason why we have to fight while still loving each other.

Martin was a straight A student at school, always at the top of his class.

On September 20, 1944, after skipping two full grades in high school, he entered Morehouse College at the age of 15.

You finished high school so quickly we haven't even had the chance to discuss your future yet.

What do you want to become?

I want to be a doctor or lawyer.

I followed your grandfather's footsteps and became the pastor of Ebenezer Baptist Church.

It was a great joy to live a life of embracing the word of God.

I hope you will consider becoming a minister too, and follow in my footsteps.

Really?

I, I'll think about it.

I'm sorry. Even though I've grown up in the church and know the Bible well, I still don't have firm beliefs about religion.

Seeing that you're slow to answer, I think you probably need some more time to think about it.

Take some time to make your decision.

Okay.

Although originally hesitant to become a minister, through discussions with Dr. Benjamin Mays, the President of Morehouse College, and Professor George Kelsey, who taught philosophy and religion, Martin slowly began to change his mind.

It's not enough to just teach blacks to be tolerant of discrimination.

Through the transfer of knowledge, education is the most precise method of enlightening both society and the individual.

Around this time Martin befriended Walter McCauley, with whom he found he could talk candidly about things.

Thus, black churches must teach the truth to help blacks become free.

Oh!

That was a great lecture. I agree with the professor completely. Ha ha ha!

A noble pastor just like my father is exactly the kind of adult I would like to become.

Then don't hesitate. Make up your mind.

…

Hmm... Religion is not an academic field, but a question of faith. I won't hesitate any longer.

Dad! I've decided to become a minister.

That's great. But you need to know that you won't become a minister automatically just because you want to.

You have to prove that your own faith can influence the faith of others.

Martin gave his first sermon at the age of 17 at Ebenezer Baptist Church, where his father was the preacher.

Every single one of you here today is one of God's children.

God is not far away. He's together with us right now, at this very moment.

We must always remember this blessing and live a life of constant gratitude.

Clap Clap Clap

Hallelujah!

Amen!

49

03

Gandhi and Non-Violent Resistance

CD1 Track 21 ▶

Martin did a number of odd jobs during his college vacations, and once again he encountered racial discrimination.

Be careful, sir!

Thanks, son.

Hey, Negroes! If you've got time to help someone else out then you can do your own job that much harder.

My name's not "Negro". It's Martin Luther King.

After working at a number of places during the vacation, I learned that racial discrimination exists in all areas of society.

Workers are verbally abused, beaten, given less wages; it's beyond description.

It's really that bad?

Hearing that even makes us feel sorry.

Let's all work together to solve the problem of racial discrimination.

Wow, I didn't know there were white people who also felt that way.

So it will be important to find whites to work together who are aware of these problems.

Exactly! Is there really any need to cooperate with an unjust system?

Incredible. So it's possible to resist without resorting to violence!

Wow.

You think this is your own bedroom or something? Be quiet!

Oops, Sorry!

What's this all about?

It's almost time to graduate and say goodbye to good old Morehouse College.

They probably think all blacks are lazy, if they believe the stereotypes. I've got to prove them wrong...

With the aim of representing black people, Martin was always well-behaved and observed proper etiquette.

If I am to keep them from drawing such conclusions, I have to always be careful of my actions.

At Crozer Theological Seminary, Martin stayed up all night reading books.

Hey, look over there!

The books we want to read never seem to be available.

Someone must be reading these books nonstop.

Plato, Aristotle, Rousseau, Hobbes, Bentham, Mill, Locke…

He's got all of the books we wanted to borrow.

Even after that first encounter with Jim, Martin remained on speaking terms with him. As time went on, Jim also warmed to being friends with Martin.
By the time they graduated they had become very close friends.

I just wanted to scare you. The gun wasn't even loaded.

Did you really plan to use that gun?

I'm gonna relax with some books.

It's Christmas break. Aren't you going out?

His holiday is reading books.

See you later.

There are so many books I want to read, there's no time to play.

I wonder if somewhere inside all these books there is anything that will help the cause of blacks?

They're all written from the perspective of whites.

60

I want to find something that will help blacks wake up, giving them life!

Around this time Martin had the chance to hear a talk given by President Johnson of Howard University.

While traveling around India for the past 50 days, I've been learning all about Gandhi.

At this talk, Martin learned about Gandhi's philosophy of non-violent resistance, which made a deep impression on him.

And Gandhi said this: "To achieve freedom, blood must flow like a river. The blood, however, must be our own."

Wow!

Hey!

Now just where do they think they are? Don't take any order from those blacks.

Yes, sir!

Why isn't the staff coming to take our order?

Do we have to go place it ourselves?

Please leave right now!

I beg your pardon?

I said leave. You wanna argue?

But we haven't done anything wrong.

Is it because we're black?

64

Hmm, surely they won't be harmed because of us?

All we wanted was a nice drive, and now I feel terrible. Let's go home.

Good idea.

The restaurant owner who threatened Martin and his friends with a gun was prosecuted by the NAACP (National Association for the Advancement of Colored People) according to the law of the state of New Jersey.

However, the lawsuit was later dismissed because the three Penn State University students refused to testify.

He must have threatened to do something to those guys if they testified.

Did you see that? Nobody's gonna testify on your behalf. Ha ha!

This can't be!

Discrimination against blacks is so deeply rooted it even supersedes the law.

Things can't continue like this!

Somebody has to take the initiative to break down the wall of discrimination that has formed deep in the hearts of white people.

With the solution to racial discrimination still eluding him, Martin Luther King graduated from Crozer Theological Seminary in June 1951, at the top of his class.

Congratulations! This car is your graduation present.

Wow!

Thank you, Dad!

Martin graduated with honors and received a scholarship of 1,200 dollars.

Ha ha ha! I bought that car with the money already set aside for you.

That means you're looking at what you were to get in tuition!

Now that you're finished with school you can return to the church to take on pastoral duties.

Actually…

I got a scholarship, so from now on I can support myself at graduate school! Ha ha ha!

What?

I got this present for nothing!

That September, Martin began graduate studies at the Boston University School of Theology, well known for its progressive divinity and philosophy departments.

So this is Boston University.

There are many professors that I respect teaching here.

They have helped me develop a deeper understanding of religion, and now I'll get to hear their lectures directly.

God represents so many special things in life. From him we can understand the process of struggle and growth.

God is the embodiment of love.

And that love is the very process of all the suffering and redemption experienced by man.

Professor Brightman's theories are so wonderful.

He makes me want to reconsider dignity and the value of man.

Coretta was greatly interested in social problems and active in social movements. Martin knew at first sight they were destined to be together.

04 .The Montgomery Bus Boycott

CD1 Track 34 ▶

What's on your mind?

Once I finish writing my doctoral dissertation I'll have to find a job, but I haven't decided what I want to do yet.

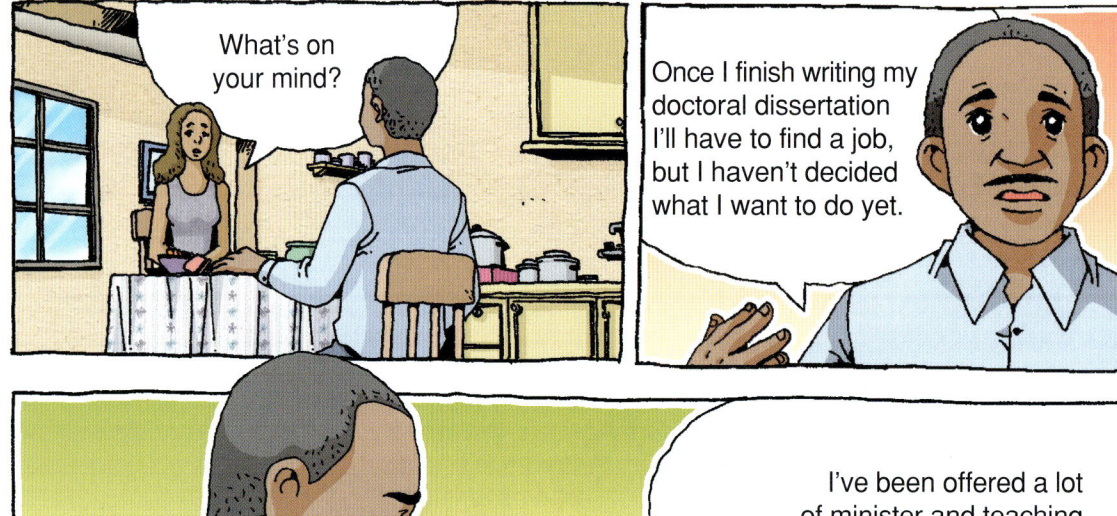

I've been offered a lot of minister and teaching positions, but I can't seem to make up my mind.

Choose what you like and can do well.

In January 1954,
Martin Luther King visited
Montgomery, Alabama.

I don't know if it's because of its long history, but this city is really beautiful.

There's the state capitol building.

I'm starting to look forward to living here.

Reverend Martin Luther King?

Yes?

We welcome you to Dexter Avenue Baptist Church.

Oh!

Martin Luther King accepted the offer to preach at Dexter Avenue Church. His first series of sermons was titled *The Three Dimensions of a Complete Life.*

There are three dimensions to any complete life: length, breadth, and height.

So does it mean height then?

The length of life does not refer to simply how long you live.

It is that inward concern that causes one to push forward, to achieve his own goals and ambitions.

Hey, be quiet!

The breadth of life is the outward concern for the welfare of others, and the height of life is the upward reach for God.

He really is good!

One month later, Martin Luther King was appointed full-time pastor of Dexter Avenue Church.

It's a letter announcing your appointment as an official pastor.

That's good news.

Actually, I had wanted to go teach at a university…

If, a few years down the road, a university offers you a job then you can go teach. How does that sound?

You're exactly right. Now why didn't I think of that? Ha ha ha!

Thanks, Coretta!

And I'm sorry for making us move south, where racial discrimination is so severe.

I just couldn't bring myself to ignore all the young people suffering here in the south from racial segregation.

And I'm supposed to be protecting you from all harm.

Don't worry about me.

You are the one who, as pastor of a southern church, will have to deal with difficulty and sacrifice.

Of course that's a responsibility I have to take.

On October 31, 1954, Martin assumed the post of pastor of Dexter Avenue Church.

In front of a congregation of around 100, Martin's father, Reverend King, gave a sermon in celebration of his son's new post.

We had planned for my son, I mean Reverend King, to come and preach at our Ebenezer Church, but he was kidnapped.

HaHaHaHa

Dad, I've followed in your footsteps to get this far. Please pray for your son as he takes his first steps on his own.

81

On December 1, 1955, something happened that would change the course of *King's life.

SCREECH

Rosa Parks, a black female secretary at the Montgomery chapter of the NAACP, refused to give up her bus seat to a white person.

Hey! A white person has boarded, so get up!

I'm exhausted after a hard day at work, and I'm supposed to give up my seat?

Both whites and blacks have to pay the same bus fare, so this is totally unfair!

*From here on Martin Luther King is referred to as simply "King"

The Kings had welcomed their first daughter, Yolanda, into the family and were living happily.

Yolanda, peek-a-boo!

Good! And how about this!

Ha ha ha! She really likes it when I do that.

Ga ga!

Why are you scaring her?

Oo-hoo!

Waaaaaa!

There's someone on the phone for you.

Yes, this is Martin Luther King.

Hello. I'm Edgar Nixon of the NAACP.

*Boycott: The refusal by a group of people to do an activity.

We should get religious leaders and citizens together to discuss this issue.

Okay. Everyone can meet at our church.

The next day various black community leaders gathered at Dexter Avenue Church to begin discussing a possible bus boycott.

I am Reverend Bennett, president of Montgomery's Interdenominational Ministerial Alliance.

We don't have much time. We should plan a bus boycott starting as early as Monday.

Rev. King, we need you along with a few more people to draft a statement.

Okay.

What are those blacks doing?

It's gotta be related to that bus boycott they're planning.

I doubt that will happen. Who wants to get sore legs walking all the way to work?

Yeah, you're right.

Just wait and see. In no time they'll be begging us to let them back on. Ha ha ha!

The first day of the boycott, December 5th, finally arrived.

Here we go…

After King's inaugural speech, the Montgomery Improvement Association proceeded to make resolutions for the direction the boycott would take in the days to come.

We resolve the following: The bus boycott will continue until we are guaranteed equal treatment by bus drivers.

We request that all passengers be allowed to sit in the order in which they boarded the bus, with whites filling in the seats from the front and blacks from the back.

We strongly request that black bus drivers be assigned to routes where the majority of passengers are black.

Hooray for the MIA!

Wow!

Hooray for Reverend King!

I believe today's cry for justice will resound around the world, bringing hope to all who are oppressed.

Better Days Are Dawning

05

CD2 Track 01 ▶

The boycott that began with the Rosa Parks incident was carried out in full force.

Are you alright?

Oh, my!

I'm fine. If this is what it takes for my grandchildren to live in a world without discrimination, then I can deal with the discomfort.

96

However, the carpool system, operated by various volunteers, had fared much better.

Free rides. Ride as much as you want.

No thanks. We'll walk.

I don't understand why they turn us down even though our service is free.

Walking is a symbol of the movement. If we ride in cars then it's like the whites have won the fight.

Oh!

How can they be even more enthusiastic than I am?

Hey Lady, looks like you need a rest. Let me take you by car.

I'm walking for the sake of my children and grandchildren, and you say I need to take a rest?

Just get out of my way, so I can Walk by!

Ha ha ha!

Okay, okay, just don't hit me!

It didn't appear like the bus boycott would end easily. The city government decided to try negotiations first.

The reason blacks have been able to cause so much havoc is the MIA. We've got to break up that group.

The bus boycott is lasting longer than we anticipated.

Negotiate?

Yeah, City Hall wants to meet with us.

Who's your leader?

Reverend King is the head of our group.

I doubt they would have caved in so quickly. They must be up to something.

The bus boycott continued unabated, prompting the mayor to hold a city council meeting on December 17th between city employees and black community leaders.

A newspaper article has come out saying three black religious leaders met with city council members and resolved the bus boycott problem.

What?

But we're all here, so who could have negotiated on our behalf?

It's a fabrication. It's just nonsense to try to break up our organization.

What time is it?

It's 11 p.m.

A lot of people will read that article and think the boycott is over.

We've got to publish an article in tomorrow's morning paper saying that this article was false.

104

Not to be outdone, the city began using more forceful methods to keep the black citizens under control.

Those who live in the same direction as I do can ride back in my car.

Okay, Reverend!

Huh?

What's the problem?

I need to see your license.

Hey, that's Reverend King!

Oh?

107

Hate only breeds more hate. Shelter everyone with love, even your enemies.

Yes, Father.

Don't give up, no matter who or what tries to threaten you.

I will do my best.

Yes, someday our hearts will be heard.

Three days later, King experienced an actual attempt to take his life.

I'm going to attend the meeting at the First Baptist Church.

Be careful.

Vroom

Hmm?

What's that noise!

BOOM

Hurray

By the grace of God, justice will prevail.

Reverend King!

Your home has been bombed!

Dear!

I'm so happy you're both alright.

Sob!

Now they're terrorizing us with bombs! Such cruelty!

Calm down, or else you'll become no different from them.

Don't worry about us.

You're right. If I lose my temper and seek revenge, then I fall right into their trap.

We can't just do nothing. We have to fight back!

Let's fight!

No. They're just waiting for us to respond with our own violence.

An eye for an eye, a tooth for a tooth! We must retaliate!

Yeah!

Stop!

If we respond with violence, they win.

We are not mobsters. Let's be civil and put down our weapons.

True victory can be had through love alone. We have to be orderly and law-abiding citizens until the very end.

But unlike before, black citizens weren't the least bit afraid. To regain their basic human rights, they no longer feared jail, threats from the KKK, or even death.

And through such courage and sacrifice, the year-long bus boycott headed toward victory.

The Supreme Court has ruled that the bus segregation laws are unconstitutional.

Wow, could it be true?

Finally there is no more racial discrimination on buses!

We achieved true victory in our own way without resorting to violence!

Yeah!

On December 20, 1956, the city of Montgomery declared racial discrimination on buses to be illegal.

Thank you everyone! However, this is only the beginning.

06 The Continuing Struggle

Even though the Montgomery bus boycott was successful, the struggle did not end there. Retaliation by whites gradually became more violent. King published the planning behind the Montgomery bus boycott as a book called *Stride Toward Freedom*.

Congratulations, Reverend.

Thank you.

To commemorate the release of the book, he held a book signing at a department store.

Are you Reverend Martin Luther King?

Yes, and you are?

Oh!

While King was signing copies of his book, he was stabbed with a letter opener by a mentally unstable black female.

Why, why me...

118

Even President Eisenhower and Vice President Nixon sent you a card.

This card is really beautiful.

That was sent by a white female student attending White Plains High School.

A white female student?

I read in the paper of your misfortune, and of your suffering. And I read that if you had sneezed, you would have died. And I'm simply writing you to say that I'm so happy that you didn't sneeze.

There are even white students who worry about me. This must be the result of our victory achieved through non-violence.

Thank you. I'll cherish this letter.

120

On February 3, 1959, King and his wife Coretta, along with their friend Dr. Lawrence Reddick, traveled to India.

The people of India greeted King with cheers and kindness, as he was well known for practicing Gandhi's method of peaceful resistance.

We read in the paper about the Montgomery bus boycott movement and were greatly moved.

Thank you for your sympathy.

That's strange. If most people in India are poor, then why does nobody look unhappy?

Moreover, despite being poor, they don't covet the things of others, and the crime rate is very low.

I wonder what has led this many people to live happily for so long?

Yeah, I had no idea there were such beautiful places.

King gained many things from his short trip to India.

With both mind and body now settled after the exhausting, long-lasting Montgomery resistance movement, King resolved to continue the fight against injustice.

I've got to fight to create a world without spite, hate, or violence. That's the only way to put a smiles on the faces of all people.

After returning from India, King accepted an offer from the Southern Religious Leaders Conference and left Montgomery, where he had worked for five years, to go to work in Atlanta.

Why did that troublemaker King come here?

Welcome to Atlanta!

Welcome, Reverend King!

If we don't deal with this properly there's bound to be trouble here too.

Some felt threatened by King's arrival, and began their attacks on him.

We charge that Reverend King falsified his tax returns while he was living in Montgomery.

He may act important but in the end King is nothing special.

There's no telling how much money he's stolen.

There's no way Reverend King could have done that!

Heh heh heh!

The case lasted four days, and with the court consisting of judge, prosecutor, and jurors, who were all white, King was at a great disadvantage.

Don't worry. Justice will certainly prevail.

Despite the odds being against him, King was acquitted of the charge.

We, the jury, find Martin Luther King not guilty of the accused charge.

Serves you right for debasing Reverend King with such a ridiculous charge!

We won! Long live Reverend King!

Not guilty? Impossible!

YEAH

In June 1960, Reverend King met presidential candidate John Kennedy for the first time.

Pleasure to meet you, Senator. At last we meet.

I apologize. I've been so busy lately with the election coming up.

Yes, I know. I too am quite interested in resolving this issue.

Senator! The unjust segregation laws need to be reformed right away.

Please don't hesitate to contact me anytime if you ever need help on that issue.

Well, meeting you was certainly worth the wait.

Just months following his meeting with Senator Kennedy, King was arrested in Atlanta.

You have a letter from a college student in North Carolina by the name of Blair.

What will you do?

He's planning a protest at a restaurant to reform segregation laws and is requesting my presence.

I don't have much choice. How can I ignore students who have requested my help?

Reverend King!

Thank you for coming. You don't know how much your simply being here means to us.

You've worked hard. Your efforts won't be for naught.

Arrest all the protestors!

King was arrested along with about 280 students.

Wherever I go, The police are there.

However, the restaurant owners dropped the lawsuit, and King and the students were released six days later.

I know that was tough for you.

No, you young students had it tougher than I did.

130

Not long afterward,
King would once again stand trial.

I recently moved here and haven't been able to change it. I'll change it as soon as possible.

I need to see your license.

Oh, an out of state license have we? That's against the law, and punishable by fine.

Reverend King, you need to appear in court.

Didn't you say I'd only be fined?

I looked you up, and you're still on probation.

That's crazy!

King was sentenced
to six months in jail for breaking
the law while on probation.

King was locked up in jail,
and the prison guards were
so rude they made King
feel humiliated.

Out!

What's
the matter
at this early
hour?

If I say 'out'
that means 'out'.
Now be quiet!

Where are you
taking me?

None of your business.
Now get in the car!

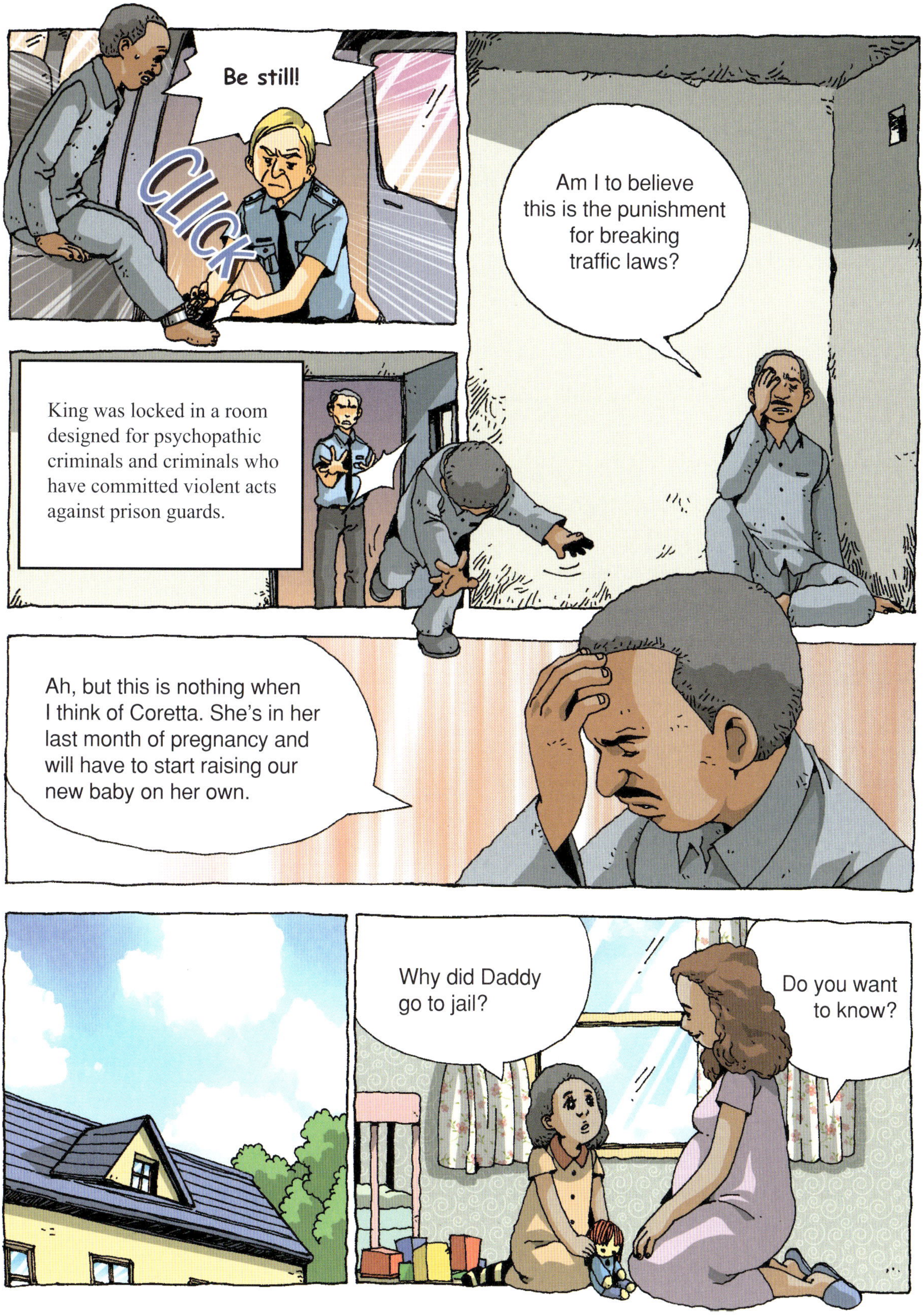

Be still!

CLICK

Am I to believe this is the punishment for breaking traffic laws?

King was locked in a room designed for psychopathic criminals and criminals who have committed violent acts against prison guards.

Ah, but this is nothing when I think of Coretta. She's in her last month of pregnancy and will have to start raising our new baby on her own.

Why did Daddy go to jail?

Do you want to know?

King was released from jail following the strong objection from Presidential candidate Kennedy.

Daddy!

You've been through so much, Dear!

I'm sorry for causing so much worry.

The following November, Kennedy was elected President of the United States with the help of overwhelming support among blacks.

Candidate Kennedy has defeated candidate Nixon to be elected the 35th President of the United States.

This is truly great news. Hopefully this will help pave the way for us blacks to live in a more peaceful society.

07 The Birmingham Children's Crusade

 Track 21 ▶

The anti-discrimination movement that started out small in Montgomery had grown, spreading to the state of Georgia. In December 1961, non-violent protests began in the form of 'Freedom Rides' in Albany, Georgia.

Discrimination still exists on public transportation vehicles that travel between states. We've got to get rid of that too.

In June 1962, King brought a number of experienced protesters into Albany to support the cause.

These people have come to help you out.

Thank you for coming.

Looks like the subjugation is already starting.

This is an illegal gathering. You're all under arrest!

Quiet!
Be quiet!

We'll pay the fine on his behalf, so please arrange for the release of King.

Yes, sir.

Now that King's in jail, the black prisoners seem more empowered.

I believe you're right.

Restaurants that accepted both white and black diners started popping up everywhere, and even public places like theaters and parks started opening their doors to blacks.

Companies that hired both whites and blacks also slowly increased in number.

However, there were still many places that stubbornly resisted desegregation. Birmingham was one such place.

Finally, our time has come.

I think we should focus our energy on ending segregation in Birmingham.

Winning in Birmingham won't be easy.

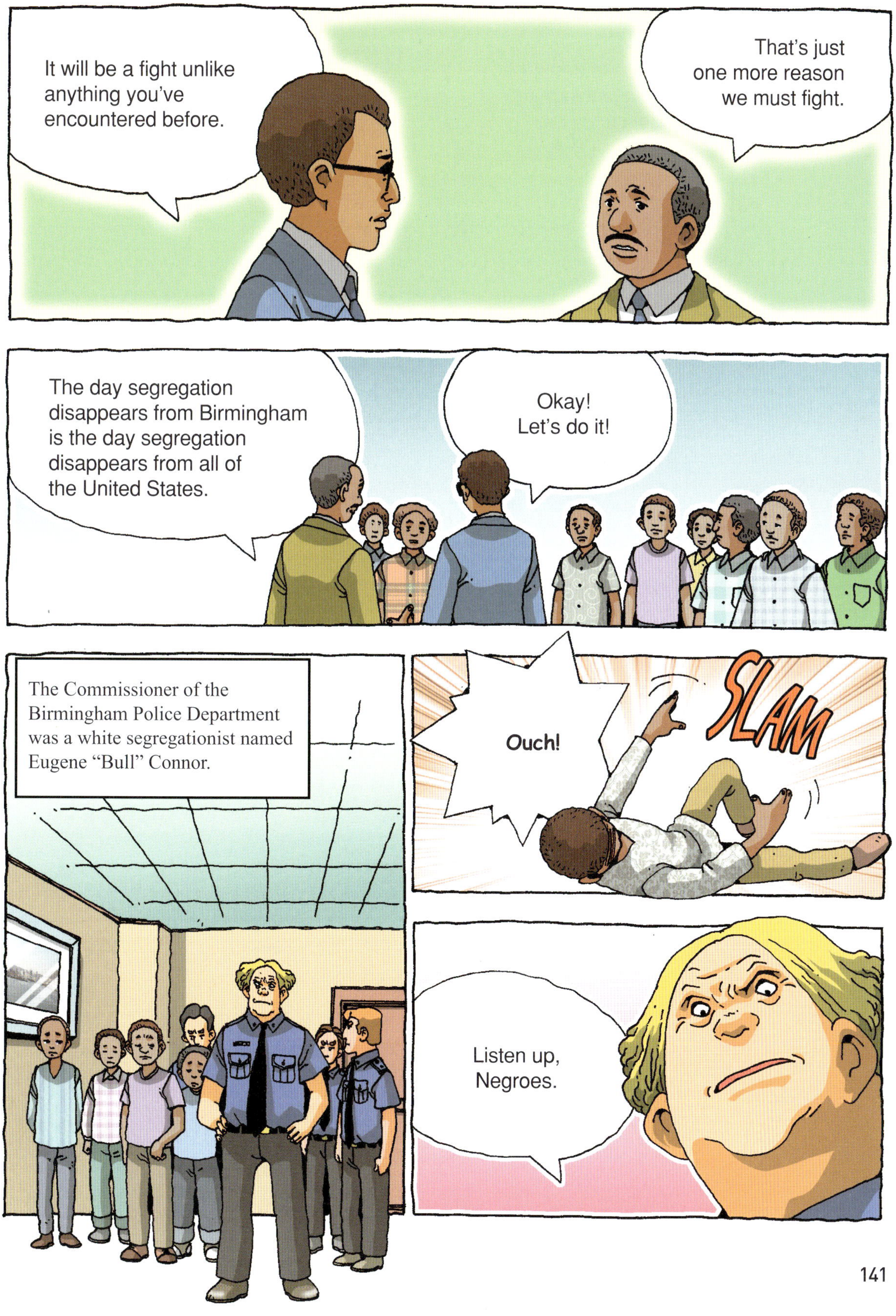

It will be a fight unlike anything you've encountered before.

That's just one more reason we must fight.

The day segregation disappears from Birmingham is the day segregation disappears from all of the United States.

Okay! Let's do it!

The Commissioner of the Birmingham Police Department was a white segregationist named Eugene "Bull" Connor.

Ouch!

SLAM

Listen up, Negroes.

141

143

Birmingham has elected a new mayor. And now there are protests happening on a scale difficult for us to keep under control.

We will not tolerate the disturbances caused by Reverend King and other outside forces.

I knew we could depend on the Bull.

But the blacks' demonstrations in Birmingham could not be taken lightly. Despite Commissioner Bull's strong efforts to suppress them, the protests continued unabated.

Be with us, God. Be with us~

Heh heh!

..please, God!

Arrest them all!

Grr

Grr

Grr

King's response, titled, 'Letter from a Birmingham Jail,' was published in the newspaper through his lawyer.

We have waited for more than 340 years for our constitutional and God-given rights.

I can't believe he's writing such garbage instead of reflecting on his behavior!

But this doesn't change anything.

A few days later, with the help of his lawyers, King was released from jail.

It's gonna be a tough fight. Neither Commissioner 'Bull' Connor or the city officials are budging an inch.

I expected this much difficulty.

Acting on a peer's suggestion, King allowed children to participate in the protests.

146

Newspapers and TV stations spread news of the suppression of the protests, enraging many people around the world.
President Kennedy was also shocked.

The events happening at Birmingham are very saddening. I think I can understand why blacks are so angry.

These words by President Kennedy greatly helped the blacks protesting in Birmingham.

Freedom

The Birmingham police gathered up the protesters daily and sent them to jail, only to find that even more protesters had come to take their place the next day.

They keep coming no matter how much we block them.

Go home! Go home so no one else gets hurt!

151

The little children pulled through. These demonstrations were more moving than all the others.

The leaders of Birmingham met with King and agreed to the demands of the black citizens.

The deep-rooted racial discrimination in Birmingham began to gradually disappear thanks to the efforts of the child protesters.

The Birmingham movement not only showed that the power of the soul was stronger than that of the body, but it also stirred the conscience of all Americans.

08 I Have a Dream

 Track 30 ▶

One month after the Birmingham struggle ended in victory for blacks, Kennedy introduced powerful legislation to the U.S. Congress.

Finally, a bill granting basic citizen rights for blacks has been submitted.

President Kennedy really made a huge decision.

It's still too early to get excited though.

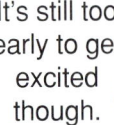

We've got to work to ensure that the bill actually passes through Congress. Let's begin assembling in Washington.

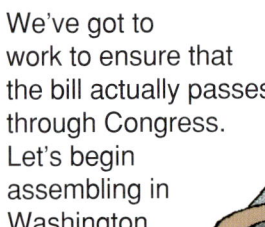

The march on Washington involved the participation of 250,000 people, more than 10 times the anticipated number.

Five score years ago, a great American signed the Emancipation Proclamation.

This momentous decree came as a great beacon of hope to millions of Negro slaves who had been seared in the flames of withering injustice.

My friends! I have a dream.

I have a dream where black men and white men will be able to join hands and let freedom ring.

YEEAAAH

When we let freedom ring from every village and every hamlet, every state and every city,

1963 was a joyous year in which civil rights legislation was introduced in Congress granting basic citizen rights to blacks. However, it was also a sad year in which precious lives were regrettably taken.

Reverend Medgar Evers has been shot and killed.

What?

A fellow civil rights activist was assassinated, while a bomb exploded inside a Birmingham church, killing four young girls.

Then, in November 1963, President Kennedy was assassinated.

Th-, This can't be.

Ah!

Oh my! How could such a thing happen?

I'm sure he's with God.

The KKK,
a white supremacy group,
was behind the Birmingham
church bombing that killed
the young girls.

The city of St. Augustine,
Florida, had become
the largest hotbed of
KKK activity.

There, white segregationists were
increasingly committing brutal,
indiscriminate acts of violence
on a scale far surpassing what had
occurred in Birmingham.

King, risking his life, proceeded
to lead the resistance movement,
and through the effort of numerous
black citizens the situation in
St. Augustine improved over time.

Fighting nonstop in the civil rights movement took a toll on King's health. Heeding the advice of those around him, he took a brief break from his activity.

You've become quite weak. A good rest will help you get better.

Ring Ring

Hello?

Honey, you've been selected as a recipient of the Nobel Prize.

On December 10, 1964, King was granted the Nobel Peace Prize.

The Nobel Prize? Did you say I'm to get the Nobel Prize?

Congratulations!

That prize is not something I should receive as an individual.

The prize should go to all the people who fought in the struggle for freedom and equality.

However, I'm extremely happy they recognized my belief that true peace can only be achieved through non-violence.

I feel an even greater burden of responsibility now.

Dear! You've already become an honorable leader of black society.

I know you will continue to do the same from now on.

On February 21, 1965, Malcom X, another black civil rights activist, was assassinated.

We've lost yet another valuable black leader.

Still, we must not respond to these acts with violence of our own.

On February 25, 1967,
at the Los Angeles Hilton, King gave
a speech wholly denouncing the U.S.
involvement in the Vietnam War.

**This war which has
destroyed the souls of
Americans and killed
countless Vietnamese
children is not
a just war.**

We must immediately end
all bombing in Vietnam.

Why is he opposing
a war we are winning?

King was criticized by those in favor of
the Vietnam War.

Shouldn't he be
paying attention to
his own civil rights
problems?

The Reverend is right.
Military force is not
the answer.

King's opposition to U.S. policy also made him a thorn in the side of politicians.

Reverend King is against the Vietnam War, right?

Right.

He's probably got another secret scheme up his sleeve.

Get the FBI to start following King's every move.

Yes sir.

King began receiving invitations to give speeches all around the country and became very busy. At his speech at the University of Berkeley a student even suggested that he run for president.

We support Reverend King! We want to send you to the White House.

To the White House!

I am only a preacher who wants to spread the word of God and fight for black civil rights.

I have no intention of entering politics.

Why are you looking around like that?

Oh, it's nothing, nothing at all.

Around this time the threat of King's assassination was mounting. White supremacy groups had even started offering a reward for his head.

Someone is after me.

King suspected there was a growing threat on his life.

When I die, don't hold a big funeral, and don't spend a lot of time investigating my death. Such things matter little.

Why did he suddenly start talking about that?

Reverend, you've got a phone call.

King set off, leaving his family and their concern for his safety behind.

Dear, please be careful.

This is serious. It's good I came here.

BANG

Before giving his prepared speech and while waiting for a fellow preacher to arrive, King was shot by an assassin's bullet while standing out on his hotel room balcony.

Although the police identified white northerner James Earl Ray as King's murderer, the real culprit was not a single person, but rather the hatred and bigotry that existed in the white-controlled United States.

King's life dedicated to civil rights and peace thus came to an end. The news of his death caused widespread sadness and anger around the world. The U.S. President proclaimed King's funeral to be a state funeral where all Americans could come and pay their respects.

LIVING the DREAM
MARTIN LUTHER KING JR.

The third Monday of January was
chosen as Martin Luther King, Jr. Day,
an annual holiday for Americans to pay tribute
to this incredible man.
Reverend King's sacrifices and efforts for love
and equality live forever in the hearts of people
around the world.

Word Search

● Find the words which are hidden horizontally, vertically and diagonally.

```
Q M Z G Q M Z G Q M Z G Q Q M Z G Q M C
W S T R U G G L E N A H W W N A H W N O
E B Q J E B Q J E B Q J E E B Q J E B M
R V C K R V C K R V C K R R V C K R V M
T C D L T C D L T C D L T T C D U T C E
Y X E Q Y X E Q Y X E Q Y Y X E N Y X M
U Z V W U Z V W U Z V W U U U Z V J U Z O
I A A E I A E E I A R E I I A R U I A R
O S S R O S G V O S G R O O S G S O S A
P D S T P D H T O D H T P P D H T P D T
A F A Y A F U Y A T U Y A A F U Y A F E
S G S U S G I U S G E U S S G I U S G I
D H S I D H O I D H O I D D H O I D H O
F J I J F J T J F J T J F F J T J F J T
G K N B G K R E C I P I E N T S B G K S
H L A N H L E N H L E N H H L E N H L E
J Q T M J Q T M J Q T M J J Q T M J Q T
L W E Q L W Y Q L W Y Q L L W Y Q L W Y
Z W K F Z W K F Z W K F Z Z S U F F E R
X E M U X E M U X E M U X X E M U X E M
C R Q C C R Q C P L I G H T R Q C C R Q
```

struggle	commemorate	devote	plight
assassinate	recipient	unjust	suffer

Vocabulary

● Match each word to the correct meaning.

1. congress	• 관용
2. institute	• 인종차별
3. ambition	• 의회
4. hate crime	• 제정하다
5. discrimination	• 저항
6. tolerance	• 불매하다
7. segregation	• 평등권
8. sacrifice	• 증오범죄
9. resistance	• 차별
10. boycott	• 희생하다
11. civil rights	• 항의
12. protest	• 야망

Guess What?

● Guess what he said in the blank.

This is precisely the reason why we have to fight while still loving each other.

Martin was a straight A student at school, always at the top of his class.

On September 20, 1944, after skipping two full grades in high school, he entered Morehouse College at the age of 15.

You finished high school so quickly we haven't even had the chance to discuss your future yet.

What do you want to become?

Writting Exercise

- Do you have a dream? Write about your dream.

My dream is to be a

_____

_____

_____

_____

Draw your dream.

I Have a Dream

● Martin Luther King made the historical address 'I Have a Dream' on August 28, 1963, in Washington, D.C.
You can hear his speech at Martin Luther King related internet sites such as http://www.mlkonline.net/. Read the context and listen to his speech, thinking about the historical meaning of the address.

I Have a Dream

……

I say to you today, my friends, that in spite of the difficulties and frustrations of the moment, I still have a dream. It is a dream deeply rooted in the American dream.

I have a dream that one day this nation will rise up and live out the true meaning of its creed: "We hold these truths to be self-evident: that all men are created equal."

I have a dream that one day on the red hills of Georgia the sons of former slaves and the sons of former slave owners will be able to sit down together at a table of brotherhood.

I have a dream that one day even the state of Mississippi, a desert state, sweltering with the heat of injustice and oppression, will be transformed into an oasis of freedom and justice.

I have a dream that my four children will one day live in a nation where they will not be judged by the color of their skin but by the content of their character.

I have a dream today.

I have a dream that one day the state of Alabama, whose governor's lips are presently dripping with the words of interposition and nullification, will be transformed into a situation where little black boys and black girls will be able to join hands with little white boys and white girls and walk together as sisters and brothers.

I have a dream today.

I have a dream that one day every valley shall be exalted, every hill and mountain shall be made low, the rough places will be made plain, and the crooked places will be made straight, and the glory of the Lord shall be revealed, and all flesh shall see it together.

This is our hope. This is the faith with which I return to the South. With this faith we will be able to hew out of the mountain of despair a stone of hope. With this faith we will be able to transform the jangling discords of our nation into a beautiful symphony of brotherhood. With this faith we will be able to work together, to pray together, to struggle together, to go to jail together, to stand up for freedom together, knowing that we will be free one day.

......

Let freedom ring from the snowcapped Rockies of Colorado!

Let freedom ring from the curvaceous peaks of California!

But not only that; let freedom ring from Stone Mountain of Georgia!

Let freedom ring from Lookout Mountain of Tennessee!

Let freedom ring from every hill and every molehill of Mississippi. From every mountainside, let freedom ring.

When we let freedom ring, when we let it ring from every village and every hamlet, from every state and every city, we will be able to speed up that day when all of God's children, black men and white men, Jews and Gentiles, Protestants and Catholics, will be able to join hands and sing in the words of the old Negro spiritual, "Free at last! free at last! thank God Almighty, we are free at last!"

연표

1929년
1월 15일, 미국 애틀랜타에서 마이클(나중에 마틴으로 이름을 바꿈) 루터 킹 1세와 앨버타 윌리엄스의 아들로 태어났습니다.

1944년 15세
조지아 주 더블린에서 열린 웅변대회에서 '흑인과 헌법'이라는 주제로 연설을 해 입상합니다.
모어하우스 대학에 입학하였습니다.

1948년 19세
모어하우스 대학에서 사회학 학사 학위를 받았습니다.
펜실베이니아 주 체스터 크로저 신학교에 입학합니다.

1951년 22세
크로저 신학교에서 신학 학사 학위를 받았습니다.
보스턴 대학 신학과에 입학하였습니다.

1953년 24세
앨라배마 주 마리온에서 코레타 스콧과 결혼합니다.

1954년 25세
앨라배마 주 몽고메리의 덱스터 애브뉴 침례교회의 목사로 취임합니다.

1955년 26세
보스턴 대학에서 신학 박사 학위를 받았습니다.
첫 아이 욜란다 데니스가 태어났습니다.
로사 파크스 부인이 흑백 분리 법률을 위반한 죄로 체포됩니다.
몽고메리 진보 연합의 회장으로 선출됩니다.

1956년 27세
자택이 테러로 폭파됩니다.
연방 최고 법원이 버스 내 흑백 분리 법률이 위헌이라고 선언합니다.
몽고메리 진보 연합의 승차 거부 운동이 끝나고 킹 목사가 흑백 통합 버스에 최초로 승차합니다.

1957년 28세 남부 기독교 지도자 회의의 의장으로 선출됩니다.
마틴 루터 킹 3세가 태어났습니다.

1958년 29세 뉴욕 할렘에서 어느 정신 질환자의 칼에 피습당합니다.

1959년 30세 가족과 함께 간디의 나라 인도를 방문합니다.

1961년 32세 셋째 아이 덱스터 스콧이 태어났습니다.

1963년 34세 넷째 아이 버니스 앨버틴이 태어났습니다.
흑인의 고용과 자유 쟁취를 위한 워싱턴 행진을 하며
'나에게는 꿈이 있습니다'라는 유명한 연설을 합니다.

1964년 35세 〈1964년 시민권 법령〉 제정으로 흑인들이 투표권을 갖게 됩니다.
오슬로에서 노벨 평화상을 수상하였습니다.

1965년 36세 앨라배마 주 셀마 시에서 투표권 쟁취를 위한 시위를 주도합니다.

1967년 38세 뉴욕 리버사이드 교회에서 최초의 공식적인 베트남 전쟁
반대 연설을 합니다.

1968년 39세 폭력으로 중단된 멤피스 시위 행진을 주도합니다.
4월 4일, 멤피스 로레인 모텔에서 괴한의 총격에 암살당합니다.

1986년 57세 미국 의회는 매년 1월 셋째 주 월요일을 킹 목사의 탄생을 기념하는
국경일로 지정합니다.

NOTE

who? 01	Barack Obama	978-89-6370-514-9
who? 02	Charles Darwin	978-89-6370-515-6
who? 03	Bill Gates	978-89-6370-516-3
who? 04	Hillary Clinton	978-89-6370-517-0
who? 05	Stephen Hawking	978-89-6370-518-7
who? 06	Oprah Winfrey	978-89-6370-519-4
who? 07	Steven Spielberg	978-89-6370-520-0
who? 08	Thomas Edison	978-89-6370-521-7
who? 09	Abraham Lincoln	978-89-6370-522-4
who? 10	Martin Luther King, Jr.	978-89-6370-523-1
who? 11	Louis Braille	978-89-6370-439-5
who? 12	Albert Einstein	978-89-6370-440-1
who? 13	Jane Goodall	978-89-6370-441-8
who? 14	Walt Disney	978-89-6370-442-5
who? 15	Winston Churchill	978-89-6370-443-2
who? 16	Warren Buffett	978-89-6370-444-9
who? 17	Nelson Mandela	978-89-6370-445-6
who? 18	Steve Jobs	978-89-6370-446-3
who? 19	J. K. Rowling	978-89-6370-447-0
who? 20	Jean-Henri Fabre	978-89-6370-448-7
who? 21	Vincent van Gogh	978-89-6370-449-4
who? 22	Marie Curie	978-89-6370-450-0
who? 23	Henry David Thoreau	978-89-6370-451-7
who? 24	Andrew Carnegie	978-89-6370-452-4
who? 25	Coco Chanel	978-89-6370-453-1
who? 26	Charlie Chaplin	978-89-6370-454-8
who? 27	Ho Chi Minh	978-89-6370-455-5
who? 28	Ludwig van Beethoven	978-89-6370-456-2
who? 29	Mao Zedong	978-89-6370-457-9
who? 30	Kim Dae-jung	978-89-6370-458-6